I0530041

Four Short Plays

Maggie Clark
Mariah Romero
Rachael Culpepper
Tristianne Dorenkamp

Presented at:
Connie Gotsch Theater
School of Arts & Humanities
San Juan College

Artemesia
Publishing

ISBN: 978-1-963832-46-4 (paperback) / 978-1-963832-47-1 (ebook)

Artemesia Publishing
9 Mockingbird Hill Rd
Tijeras, New Mexico 87059
info@artemesiapublishing.com
www.apbooks.net

Dedication

To Connie Gotsch who was an advocate of the arts in the Four Corners region and in developing young minds. All of the plays in this book were performed at the Connie Gotsch Theater located on the campus of San Juan College.

A Note from Professor Eric R. Arpelar

This was one of the greatest semesters of college theatre arts that I have been a part of in my career. I have seen the talents of students be exploited, and these four students will work in this business, and they will also be very successful. In this course of Theatre Arts, each assignment led into this final. The class began with students doing pantomime and stage combat performances, and these elements had to be incorporated into the play that they would scribe for their playwriting project that was also their midterm assignment. From that point, they all did directorial projects that showcased how they would conduct an audition process, a rehearsal schedule, and a performance schedule format. Then, as their last assignment, they did a theater business project that showcased how they would develop and roll out a theatrical season for a theater company or events center. They had to create a budget with parameters, and one of the major objectives is they had to stay within that budget and also come in at the end of the season in the black. These plays, their conception, production, direction, and performance, are a cumulation of all the student exploitation of talents and hard work this semester. And, because of that, we have four plays that are all unique in their own right and yet all showcase the style of creativity that these students exhibit.

Magdalene J. Clark is the writer and the director of Good-Bye for Now. Ms. Clark is an experienced and seasoned stage manager and technical stagehand. With that, she has dreams and aspirations of being a stage director, and in this case, what a way to start a career with a student-written play in college with a world premiere that she not only directed but also wrote. Ms. Clark has such a passion for stage management and directing that she will not only work in this business but also be a game changer as well.

Tristianne Dorenkamp is the writer and director of Two-Faced Spies. Ms. Dorenkamp is a seasoned actress, podcaster, and a published artist. She is a massive creative, and she also has an administrative mindset where she could be a driving force in the business aspect of business. With her experience and education to come, Tristianne will also be a driving force in this industry for years to come.

Mariah Romero is the writer and director of The Dilemma. Ms. Romero is an experienced actress in the Four Corners, and she is constantly seeking roles that constantly build her acting reputation. She is extremely versatile in her acting, and she will definitely be someone that we will see in the future. With this world premiere, she is building her résumé that will one day be one among award winners.

Rachael Culpepper is the writer and director of They Did What? Mrs. Culpepper is a seasoned actress and currently a business administration major at San Juan College. She has dreams of opening up her own local theatre company in the future. This dream was brought into fruition, especially when she did her theatre business presentation and showcased her season that she would bring for her theatre company. With Rachael, you definitely see advertisements in the future of her community theater and the creative seasons that she brings to the community.

As you read these plays or you decide to perform them, you will want to remember these names: Clark, Dorenkamp, Romero, and Culpepper. Reason being, those reading it can know it is possible to work in this business and exploit their talents. As a professor, there is nothing more exhilarating than seeing students succeed and bring their talents to the world.

Eric R. Arpelar
Adjunct Professor of Film & Theatre
School of Arts & Humanities
San Juan College

Contents

GOOD BYE FOR NOW

WRITTEN AND DIRECTED BY
MAGGIE CLARK

ONE LETTER... ONE GIANT
DECISION

Good Bye For Now

A play in 1 act

By Maggie Clark

CHARACTERS

JESSE: Leading Male character, in love with Lauren, confused in what he wants in life.

LAUREN: Strong independent woman but has a soft spot for Jesse, wanting her ideal life to play out with Jesse.

CHELSEA: Laurens Best friend and her support system through everything.

MARK: The mail man.

SETTING

A Movie Theater Lobby

TIME

Evening Mid 1980's

ACT I

SCENE 1

(Lauren, Jesse and Chelsea walk out of a movie theater into the Lobby)

Jesse

Geez Chelsea I've never seen anyone jump that high before.

Chelsea

Oh, shut it. I saw your popcorn go flying too.

Lauren

Next time, seriously, let me pick the movie

Jesse

No way, then we will be stuck watching chick flicks forever.

(Chelsea Looks around at the movie posters on the wall)

Chelsea

Come on we could have seen the new Superman movie. That would have been amazing.

Lauren

Seriously, Jesse, what were you thinking about with that movie.

Jesse

Hey, we have to have one last fun memory before college who knows what's going to happen.

Chelsea

Wow, wow, Jess don't talk like that we literally all are going to the same school. Nothings gonna change.

Jesse

Yea, you're right.

Chelsea

Come on don't be a buzz kill. Lighten up. What's our plan for tomorrow?

(Friendly punches him on the shoulder.)

Lauren

Well, move in is at six so we need to leave around twelve so we can make it and have fun on the way right, Jess?

Jesse

Yea right. Twelve.

Lauren

Okay then... well, are you all packed, Chelsea?

Chelsea

Well, yes and no. My mom was supposed to go through my closet with me today but... here I am.

Lauren

How 'bout you, Jess?

Jesse

Yup. I've been packed sense like July

Lauren

Yea me too! I'm so excited guys. Tomorrow is gonna be the best day ever.

Jesse

Of course it is. I mean we've been dreaming about this sense we were what, like nine.

Chelsea

Seriously. I feel like it was just yesterday we were chasing around the playground, going to camp together. It's always been us three. I seriously couldn't be more grateful for you two.

Lauren

No, I know. I don't know what I would have done, I can't imagine high school with anyone else. I mean me and Chelsea on the sidelines while you bring the school to state champs, Jess. I mean, gosh it's so perfect and now college, it's going to be such a dream. Right Jess?

Jessie

(In a lying tone)

Yea. I mean we are gonna do everything we can't do now. Late nights together when we should be doing homework. Midnight snack runs. God knows what else we will come up with. It's going to be amazing.

Chelsea

Are you sure you're okay Jess?

Jessie

Yeah, I am just thinking a lot about everything right now.

Lauren

I get it, Jess. It's gonna be a hard change but just think about how amazing it's going to be.

(She grabs his arm to hold him, and he stands stiff)

(There is an awkward amount of silence)

Chelsea

Well anyways, I'm really glad we were able to do something one last time back at home where it all started.

(stopped by a Mailman approaching Jesse)

Mark

Jesse Morris. I believe this letter is for you

(Hands a letter to Jesse)

Jesse

Couldn't it wait?

Mark

Um... I was across the street at your mother's, but she told me to bring it to you as soon as I could. I have to go now.

(Mark looks at Jesse sorrowfully and Exits)

Lauren

What is that, Jess?

Chelsea

Ooo... your secret admirer.

Lauren

Oh, shut it Chelsea... Well, open it, Jess

(Jesse Takes a step back and opens the letter)

(A pantomime takes place as he reads that he got into the military school he applied to behind Laurens back)

Lauren

God Jess ,what is it!?

(She grabs the letter while he tries to pull it away, but finally lets her take it.)

You told me you didn't even apply! How could you!?

Chelsea

What's happening, Jesse. What did you do?

Jesse

(Goes to grab Lauren to hug her but she shoves him off of her)

Lauren listen... It's not what you think. I—

Lauren

Save your excuses. What about us, Jess? College? Our future? Is that nothing to you!? You promised me!

Jesse

You don't get it, If I didn't apply my dad would have killed me. It doesn't mean anything, Lauren.

Chelsea

Do you guys want a minute?

Lauren

No, please stay.

(She begins to tear up)

Chelsea

You could have at least told us, man.

Jesse

I never thought I would get it. I swear I
don't want this, Lauren.

Lauren

Jess what are you going to do? What are
WE going to do? This was supposed to be
our last night as high schoolers. Our last
night before our future. What am I
supposed to do? I gave it all for you! I
didn't go to Berkley because you didn't
get in. Does that mean anything to you!

(She grabs his shirt and falls into it crying)

Jesse

(Doesn't know what to say but puts his hand
on her head)

Chelsea

Jesse, you need to say something.
Anything. Are you going to go there? All

11

the way across the country. Just leave her like this?

Jesse

Look, I don't know, Chelsea. If I go with you guys my dad will never speak to me again, I will be on my own. If I go to Maine it's over and I lose the only two people who love me, but my dad is happy. I don't know what to do.

Lauren

So, you actually are thinking about it! You don't even like your dad most the time, why do you care so much!?

Jesse

I... I don't know, Lauren, just give me time to think, okay? I have to talk to my dad and just think, okay? I know you don't get it, but this is a big decision, okay? Do you get that?

Chelsea

(Looks at her watch)

Guys, I have to go. I'm sorry. I told my mom I would be home by ten. Jesse, whatever decision you make know I'll take care of Lauren. That's my best friend. I hope you do what's right. If I don't see you again thank you for being the best brother I could ask for these past 6 years.

(She gives him a big hug and looks at Lauren with love and gives her a hug and then exits)

                    Jesse

Are you…. mad?

                    Lauren

Mad? No, I guess not. I'm upset, Jess. I always thought it was going to be us.

                    Jesse

And it can be still, Lauren. It's you. It's always gonna be you.

                    Lauren

But is it me? Or is it your dad? I just don't get why you couldn't come to me.

                    Jesse

I was doing everything so I didn't get accepted, Lauren. I don't want to go. I want to be with you and Chelsea at college. I want what we always planned.

                    Lauren

Then don't go.

                    Jesse

Would you wait?

Lauren

I can't promise that.

Jesse

I know you can't.

Lauren

I love you, Jess

Jesse

And you know I love you

I'm not gonna go. I can't leave you. My mom always told me to follow my heart. And you have my heart, Lauren.

Lauren

Don't do this to me, Jess. Your gonna go home and your dad is gonna say otherwise. It has to be over, Jess.

Jesse

I think you are right, Lauren. I am so sorry. I don't want this. I have to go. Please... Please don't hate me forever. I promise I'll come back for you.

Lauren

I love you. But you need to go now Jess.

Jessie

Let me at least walk you home?

Lauren

Fine. Then it's goodbye, ok?

Jesse

No. Its goodbye for now.

(Curtain closes)

MARIAH ROMERO'S

THE DILEMMA

CONNIE GOTSCH
THEATER
DECEMBER 13TH 7PM

The Dilemma

A play in 1 act

By Mariah Romero

CHARACTERS

JOSEPHINE: Soon to be bride

CLAUDIA: Josephine's younger sister and her maid of honor

VIVIEN: Josephine's best friend from college, one of her bridesmaids.

DIANA: Josephine's friend from college, one of her bridesmaids.

SETTING

A courtyard.

TIME

Afternoon. Sometime in the mid 1990's

ACT I

SCENE 1

(A courtyard, late afternoon. Vivien, Claudia, and Diana enter.)

Diana

Any ideas on what it's going to be about this time?

Vivien

(Annoyed)

Who knows. Everything ticks her off now. I mean she got upset with me because my skin was too pale and didn't contrast nicely with my dress, she even offered to pay for a tan.

Claudia

Come on you guys. You know she is going through a lot of stress right now, we all know this isn't our usual Josie.

(The three women see Josephine sitting at a table waving them over and they all take a seat)

Josephine

Good afternoon ladies! I'm so glad you three could make it. I have so much I need to tell you.

Diana

So, what was it you urgently needed to tell us?

Josephine

Eager are we? Anyways I wanted to discuss the wedding.

Vivien

Wow what a shocker!

Claudia

Viv! What is wrong with you?

Vivien

I'm sorry! I was only kidding Josie, what's going on?

Josephine

(Slightly glares at Vivien and then sighs)

It's Mark. Something is seriously wrong. He has totally been giving me the cold shoulder lately!

The Dilemma | Mariah Romero

Claudia

Has anything been happening between
you two lately?

Vivien

Besides the fact that you have been such
a bi—

Claudia

Vivien! Seriously you need to quit!

Josephine

It's fine Claudia, I have been rather brash
with the whole wedding planning. I just
hate it!

Mark and I were doing so good for so
long and now it's like a giant wall is built
between us.

Diana

If you want my honest opinion Josephine,
it seems you built that wall yourself.

Vivien

Yeah, I mean come on Josie, you yelled at
the dude because the engagement ring
wasn't to your standard!

Josephine

I was only upset due to the lack of effort! Every girl wants a big shiny ring on their finger!

Vivien

Then buy the ring yourself little miss stockbroker!

(Diana covers her mouth to hide her giggle)

Claudia

Excuse me?

Vivien

Oh, come on Claudia, do you always have to speak for the princess.

Josephine

This Princess can speak for herself just fine thanks. Alright Vivien since you so badly want to talk why don't you go ahead and explain to me why your panties are in such a twist!

(Vivien clenches her fists and looks into her lap)

Vivien

God Josie! You really don't see how arrogant you are, do you? I mean everything and I mean EVERYTHING is about you in some shape or form. I can't go one day without having to listen to some complaint about your oh-so-very-rough-life which—come on dude—you get everything handed to you and then Mark—

(Vivien falls silent)

Diana

(Reaches for Vivien's shoulder and gives it a rub and softly retorts.)

It's ok Viv take a deep breath.

Josephine

Mark? What about Mark, Vivien?

Vivien

(Struggling to get her words out)

Nothing! It's nothing I just think—

(A server walks in and sets some drinks down)

—Oh, thank you! Look Josie—

Josephine

(Correctively)

Josephine. You don't get to call me that anymore.

Vivien

Ok Josephine. Bottom line is, you treat your fiancé like garbage and you know what? Mark is a good guy. He's genuine, he's kind, attentive, and supportive and so many women would do anything for a guy like that and It's beginning to get to a point that he is starting to see that for himself.

(She clamps her hand over her mouth)

Diana

(Stands up and starts gathering her belongings)

I think me and Viv should get going now.

Claudia

Sit the hell down. What are you getting at, Vivien?

(Diana sheepishly sits back down and Vivien sits in silence)

Josephine

SPEAK DAMN IT!

Vivien

(Erratically and very quick)

Mark and I have been seeing each other.

(Claudia and Josephine collectively gasp)

Claudia

You've been what?!

Vivien

(Talking through tears)

I am so sorry Josephine I truly am but we just we, we get each

(Josephine stands up walking towards Vivien)

other and we both haven't felt anything like it before an—

(Josephine slaps Vivien across the face and an argument ensues. Claudia and Diana stand up moving to separate the two.)

Diana

What the hell! Grab your things Viv we need to leave.

Claudia

(Turns to Diana)

I seriously can't believe you! Did you know about all of this?

Diana

(Looks to Claudia for a moment then turns to grab her and Vivien's belongings)

I said let's go Vivien!

(Vivien walks to Diana and takes her purse. She takes a dollar bill out of her purse and places It on the table)

There you go Josie, maybe that can buy you a ring you'd like.

27

(Vivien and Diana exit. Josephine sits down aware of all of the eyes on her. She begins to cry into her hands and Claudia goes to her.)

It's all going to be alright Josie, look at me.

(Josephine looks up to Claudia with tears down her cheeks. Claudia pushes the hair out of her Josephine's face and begins to wipe her tears with the back of her hands. She fixes Josephine's hair and then kneels to grab Josephine's hands.)

You are so beautiful, you know that? To me it seems like the trash took it's self out so get up and let's go home.

Josephine

(She smiles softly and stands up and exits with Claudia.)

Presenting the World Premere of

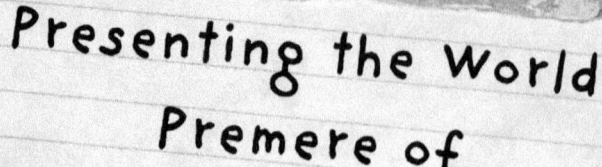

They Did What?

Written and Directed by
Rachael Culpepper

Free Student
Short Play Festival
@
The Connie Gotsch
Theater

12- 13- 2024

They Did What?

A play in I act

By Rachael Culpepper

CHARACTERS

SPENCER SPENCER: Late 20's-early 30's. Young fresh off the bar lawyer. He lives with his mom and is running a practice out of her garage. Mild-mannered and introverted but assertive when he needs to be.

KATHLEEN SPENCER: 60's. Spencer's Mom. Very bad at her job as her son's secretary and unofficial paralegal. Well-meaning. Very kind and thoughtful. She shows her love through acts of service.

LOGAN WRIGHT: Late 30's early 40's. Frenemy and neighbor of Brayden. Passive aggressive. Lower middle class is trying to live above his pay grade. Logan grew up in a low-income household, so he is envious of Brayden because of his upper-class upbringing.

BRAYDEN MILLS: Late 30's early 40's. Frenemy and neighbor of Logan. Loud and arrogant. Raised in a rich family but lives the middle-class lifestyle after he crashed too many cars on his father's dime, so he was cut off. Jealous of Logan because he married Brayden's "The one who got away."

SETTING

A garage in a suburban neighborhood. There is a desk that is actually a plastic folding table with piles of folders. There is a laptop computer on the "desk". The "desk" has a lawn chair behind it and two lawn chairs in front. There is a door leading into the main house. (located where it makes sense for KATHLEEN to come in and out of). There are a few storage boxes and an ironing board. (Digital backdrop Unfinished garage with items hanging off the walls) At the entrance of the garage there is a TV tray that is supposed to be a desk with a messy binder on top with a lawn chair behind it where the secretary sits. The overall feel of the garage is cluttered and disorganized.

TIME

After noon. Modern day July.

PROPS

Laptop with mouse, 3 cell phones, a book (or other activity), 5 lawn chairs. Garage clutter, TV tray, Folding table, files in manila folders, a candy dish, hard candies in a plastic wrapper, post-its, Ironing board, shirt with red ink stain, gaming headphones, and an intimidating looking baseball bat (bat with nails sticking out of it)

ACT I

SCENE 1

(A garage, Afternoon. SPENCER and KATHLEEN are sitting in their respective areas of "the office" SPENCER has headphones on and appears to be playing a MMO Video Game. KATHLEEN is reading a book. BRAYDEN Enters taking in the sight of the "office")

> Brayden

Hi. So, my GPS told me the Spencer Spencer Law firm office is at this address, but I think it led me to the wrong place. Do you know where to find 1616 Willow Wind Drive Suite B?

> Kathleen

This is it, you found us. Spencer Spencer Law. I'm Kathleen Spencer. *(Looks in leger)* I'm guessing you're his one o'clock. Brandon Moss?

> Brayden

(annoyed)

No BRAY-DEN MILLS. M-I-L-L-S.

Katheen

Isn't that what I said? Yep. One pm.
You're here a little early. Mr. Spencer is in
a meeting right now.

Spencer

I'm the tank, you're the DPS!!! Yes, I got
it, I got it. HEALS! Come on, come on,
come on, come on!!! HEAL me NOW!!!

Brayden

It looks to me like he's playing World of
Warcraft.

Kathleen

Semantics. They meet every weekday
from ten till one, seems like a meeting to
me. He'll be done by the time of your
meeting. So please wait in the lobby area
and I will give you a holler when the
meeting is over. Okay, sweety?

Brayden

What lobby? *(Under his breath)* You
won't have to holler that loud.

(KATHLEEN points to a folding chair and
BRAYDEN begrudgingly folds it out and sits
contemplating leaving after seeing "the
office". Logan enters garage.)

Logan

Hello, do you know where to find 1616
Willow Wind—

(notices BRAYDEN in the "lobby")

Brayden, what the damn hell?

Brayden

Yeah, this is it bro. Wait what do you
mean, 'what the damn hell'? Why are
you here, Logan?

Logan

Oh, you know. You know what you did to
me. I told you I was suing!

Brayden

What I did? What about what you did to
ME!? Well tough jerky bro I got here first,
so find your own lawyer.

Logan

What are you even doing, going to a
lawyer who advertises with phone
number slips on the gym bulletin board
like its 2001? Doesn't your family have a
lawyer?

Brayden

Don't go there, bro you know I haven't
talked to my dad since I crashed my tenth
Jag.

Logan

Dude! I'm not your bro after the shady
shit you pulled. You are going down. I
have an appointment for one pm! So, I
get to go first!

Brayden

No way! My appointment is at one! I'm
going first

Kathleen

(Flipping through the schedule book)

Oh dear. My goodness. I'm so sorry. I see
what I did wrong. I put one of you
gentlemen on the wrong Thursday, but I
told you both today's date. May I offer
you some hard candy for the trouble?

Logan & Brayden

NO!

(SPENCER done with his game walks over
and gives the gentleman a withering look for
yelling at his mom.)

Logan & Brayden

No thank you ma'am. Very, very kind of
you to offer.

Spencer

Mom, I love you, but that is the sixth
time this week. Will you please start

writing the agreed date and time under their names?

(*KATHLEEN mouths: "Sorry"*)

Hi, how are you gentlemen? Nice to meet you. This happens more than I'd like it to. So, I overheard. You're suing each other? That's a first.

(LOGAN and BRAYDEN talk all at once something about the "Block Party Incident" and who deserves to be represented and how the other guy did something waaaay worse than what I did. It was self-defense! It wasn't my fault! Improv encouraged)

Spencer

Okay….okaaaaay…Excuse me…Excuse…Me….ENOUGH!!

(SPENCER stomps his foot. LOGAN and BRAYDEN stop short looking embarrassed.)

Spencer

Awesome. Now that we are done acting like toddlers, let's come up with a game plan, okay? I have another meeting in an hour. So, I need to hear the whole story from you both. BOTH of you will take turns a few sentences at a time until the story is done. Then I'll pick one of you to represent. Got it?

(LOGAN AND BRAYDEN nod in agreement)

Spencer

Alright, step into my office and we'll get this meeting—these meetings—started.

Logan

What office?

Brayden

Well, this is the "Lobby" So I'm guessing that's the "Office?"

(He points to the makeshift office)

Kathleen

Mr. Spencer will see you now. Right this way.

(Gestures to the makeshift office area. SPENCER, LOGAN, and BRAYDEN sit on the lawn chairs.)

Spence, you haven't eaten since before your meeting. Would you like a sandwich?

Spencer

No thank you. Why don't you take a break? I can make my own sandwich later.

Kathleen

Okay, let me know if you need anything. WHAT IS THAT? ARE YOU BLEEDING?

> Spencer

I'm fine, everything is fine. It's just ink, I think a pen exploded in my pocket. It's just ink.

> Kathleen

INK? Goodness my soul just about burst through my chest. Give me the shirt, I have to get that stain out.

> Spencer

No, no thank you I gotta get this meeting started, okay. It's fine. I'll give it to you when the meeting is over.

(KATHLEEN crosses over to SPENCER and gestures for him to give her the shirt with a mom face on)

> Kathleen

Red is so hard to get out I need to soak it soon. Hand it over.

(SPENCER shakes his head and non-verbally protests as his mom tries to unbutton his shirt)

> Logan

She's right dude, the longer it sits on there the harder it is to get out.

(SPENCER takes off his shirt and is now wearing an undershirt. KATHLEEN takes the shirt and EXITS (door into house)

41

Spencer

Sorry about that gentleman. Let's get
started, how about you go first?

(Points at LOGAN)

Brayden

Hey, I was here first! Shouldn't I get to
start! I waited in the lobby!

Spencer

Fine. go ahead.

Brayden

Okay, so. I've been calling it the block
party incident. It was last week on the
fourth, you know, Independence Day. The
HOA asked me to grill for the block party.
It all started when—

Logan

NO dude. No. The HOA asked ME to grill
for the block party, that's why I was
already set up when you got there!

Brayden

(BRAYDEN and LOGAN shove each other.)

I thought we were taking turns!

Spencer

Hey enough with the toddler crap. We're
all adults here act like it.

(KATHLEEN enters the GARAGE)

Kathleen

Spence hon, I can't find the bottoms of your Batman Pajama's did you put them in the hamper?

Spencer

(Embarrassed)

As far as I know. I'm in a meeting, remember?

Kathleen

I know I'm just here for the ironing board. Your boxers are so wrinkled.

Spencer

Okay! Mom, please, make it quick.

(KATHLEEN gestures at the boys to hand her the ironing board. LOGAN hands it to her. SPENCER'S cell phone rings.)

Spencer

(SPENCER answers the phone and mouths sorry. KATHLEEN mouths "Oh you're on the phone? I'll go." Exits")

Spencer Spencer law firm. Spencer speaking... There is only one Spencer... I'm both Spencers... No, my secretary is a Spencer, but she's not licensed to practice... Yeah, first AND last... A 1:15

meeting? Well, I'm actually in two meetings now... No, I'm one person... Okay, you have a witness testimony for the Johnson case. Okay, I'll listen, make it quick. Uh huh.

(SPENCER Pantomimes a reaction to the witness testimony the account is very harrowing, and SPENCER is enthralled with the story and has variety of emotional reactions to the story. LOGAN opens a piece of hard candy. SPENCER glares in the direction of the men. BRAYDEN snatches up the candy and non-verbally admonishes LOGAN. SPENCER starts typing on his computer. Pantomime ends when SPENCER yells.)

Spencer

THEY DID WHAT?

What were those names again? I just need to clear up some typos. Okay...Uh huh thank you for securing that testimony. Will you have her email me a written copy of that statement? Thanks. That will be no problem. I'll take care of it. (*end of phone call*)

Okay before we get any further. I need some info for my records. Will you verify your phone numbers please?

(LOGAN and BRAYDEN give SPENCER their phone number's on paper. SPENCER types stuff out then messes with his cell phone.

The men look at each other confused. Two "airdrop" sounds happen one after the other and the men look at their cell phone.)

You just got served! Paperless filing! BOOM. You both are pieces of work you know that?! I don't know what you did to each other. And I don't care! What you did to my client? Deplorable. WOW. Just wow. At a loss for words... Truly. I am THRILLED to take you both for all that you are worth.

                    Logan

Ohhhhh

                    Brayden

THAT. Johnson... Hey, wait that's not fair, you didn't even get our side of the story!

(BRAYDEN grabs SPENCER by the collar, SPENCER wiggles out of his grip as LOGAN is rearing for a punch. SPENCER gasps and ducks down. He frantically grabs manilla folders of his desk and swats at the men. The men keep attacking SPENCER while he evades until BRAYDEN grabs ahold of SPENCER so LOGAN can punch him. KATHLEEN enters with a very intimidating bat. She lets out a deep blood curdling yell and chases the men out of the garage. After KATHLEEN shouts, SPENCER starts stacking files back on his desk)

Kathleen

GET THE HELL AWAY FROM MY SON!!!!

Spencer

That was terrifying. I love you, but you are a terrible secretary. I'm going to put ads out tomorrow.

Kathleen

Good. That's all for the best. I was not looking forward to reorganizing those files.

Spencer

Yeah, yeah, I don't blame you. But can I keep you on for security?

Kathleen

Oh yeah sure thing. I heard you yelling earlier, what DID they do?

Spencer

You DO NOT want to know.

THE TWO-FACED
SPIES

A SHORT PLAY BY TRISTIANNE DORENKAMP

WHO IS THE REAL MASTERMIND?

DEC 13TH
CONNIE GOTSCH THEATRE

The Two-Faced Spies

A play in one act

By Tristianne Dorenkamp

CHARACTERS

DR. BELLA: A stern and straight-forward woman, who got her doctorate in psychology

CARLA: A free-spirit woman with a southern accent.

CHARLIE: A charming young spy with a British accent.

ATHENA: A beautiful young spy with anger issues.

SETTING

A restaurant

TIME

Evening. Some time in the 2070s

ACT I

SCENE 1

(A Restaurant called The Secret Sapphire, early evening. Athena and Charlie are sitting at a counter with some drinks. Carla and Dr. Bella enter.)

Dr. Bella

Thank you for meeting me here, Carla.

Carla

Of course, Becky Bella, oops, I mean, Dr. Bella now. All fancy with your doctorate in psychology. I'm so excited to hang out with you! Just like old times. I remember when you used to need help with homework and—

Dr. Bella

(Interrupts)

I'm afraid that is not why I called you here, sit down.

(Dr. Bella gestures to a seat, Carla sits)

Carla

Whoa, so serious, Becky, is something wrong?

Dr. Bella

Carla, you know how you were just
talking about how when we were kids,
you used to help me with homework?
However, I was one of the smartest kids
in our school, meaning you have always
been very clever.

Carla

(She smiles proudly)

I mean I could always put two and two
together, but that isn't saying much in
this day and age.

Dr. Bella

I need your help with something.

Carla

Oh... Of course, Becky. With what?

Dr. Bella

Now, don't freak out, but see those two
charming people behind me?

(Indicating Athena and Charlie)

I have been studying these two for weeks
for a... project I've been working on, but I
came to a... undesirable conclusion. I
have come to find out that those two are
some of the most dangerous people in
the world. They are the most skilled
assassins in the current era.

(Carla laughs)

I'm serious, and that isn't even the worst part! They work for enemy organizations, but they have no idea, and have been coming here together for weeks. If they ever realize... I don't want to know what's going to happen if they realize. That's why I called you. You're the smartest person I know! How can I defuse this situation before it blows up!

Carla

Dr. Bella! Your imagination has gotten the best of you! This is completely ridiculous! Here, I'll just go talk to them and show you that this is all in your head.

(Carla stands up but Dr. Bella grabs her wrist)

Dr. Bella

Carla, don't!

(Carla yanks away and starts to walk over. Dr. Bella stands up and violently gestures for Carla to sit back in her seat. Carla gestures towards Athena and Charlie and keeps walking. Dr. Bella shakes her head but Carla ignores her.)

Carla

Excuse me, Sir.

Charlie

(Charlie looks up from his conversation with Athena)

How can I help you, Madam?

Carla

Sorry, to interrupt. My friend over there seems to think you and your friend are spies for like, different companies or whatever. Can you please tell her she's being ridiculous!

(Charlie and Athena look at each other)

Athena

Well, I'm not a spy, and you are definitely not a spy, right, Charlie?

Charlie

Of course not.

(Charlie laughs as he looks over at Dr. Bella.)

Tell your friend that I work at The Three Brothers Supply Company.

Athena

Wait... you told me that you worked at Extras.

(Athena looks Charlie dead in the eyes.)

Charlie

...I can work at two places, Athena.

(Carla takes a step back)

Carla

Oh, no way. Becky was… on second thought, I think she was actually pointing at those two people over in the corner of the—

(Charlie tries to hit Athena on the side of the head with his glass but she ducks.)

Carla

Oh no!

Fight begins:

Beat 1: Athena punches Charlie in the stomach then smacks his head against the counter.

Beat 2: Charlie grabs Athena by the hair and throws her to the ground.

Charlie

Tell me who you work for, Athena. Is it the C.C.S?

Athena

Like I'd ever tell you.

Beat 3: Athena jumps up and punches him in the throat, then kicks him in the stomach.

Beat 4: Dr. Bella stands up and pulls out her phone.

Dr. Bella

Agent Sky, we have a problem.

Carla

Oh, so you're a spy too? Is that why they were your "Project?" Did you even get a degree in psychology?!

Beat 5: Charlie grabs the golf club from off the wall and tries to smack Athena in the head with it, but she catches it mid-swing.

Dr. Bella

I did get a degree in psychology! There are many uses for my field in a spy organization!

Carla

Yeah?! Like what, Becky! Do you—

Beat 6: Charlie and Athena wrestle over the golf club, Charlie ends up pushing Athena into Carla. They both fall over.

Athena

Get out of my way, you annoying slug!

(Athena stands up just as Dr. Bella gets out of her seat and pulls out a gun.)

Dr. Bella

Don't you move!

(Athena and Charlie put their hands up.)

Carla

You couldn't have done that earlier!

Athena

You're Agent Mike, and you work for
S.P.R.C! Don't you, Charlie?!

Charlie

Guilty is charged. If you don't work for C.
S. S, then it must be H.B.V? So, you must
be Agent Rose.

Athena

Lucky guess. I'm surprised you figured it
out.

Carla

(Carla sits up then pulls out a recorder from
her pocket and clicks a button)

And I'm surprised by what fools you both
are.

Charlie

What?

Dr. Bella

(Looks at Carla)

Nice work, Agent Forty-Six, and don't you
two think of trying anything. We have the
place surrounded.

Athena

You...? How did...?

Carla

Oh come on, Athena. You really think we thought you couldn't hear us talking at the table three feet away from you? We've been following you two for some time, we expected who you were, but needed vocal proof to put you behind bars, and now, we've got it.

(Dr. Bella and Carla grab the other two and cuff their hands.)

Dr. Bella

But, actually though, we really should go grab something to eat with the whole gang sometime.

Carla

Definitely.

(They all exit stage left.)

www.ingramcontent.com/pod-product-compliance
Lightning Source LLC
Chambersburg PA
CBHW071217120626
46546CB00006B/2610